ROCK CLIMBING

by Tim Seeberg

Content Advisor: Matt Semet, Senior Editor, Rock and Ice Magazine, Carbondale, Colorado

Published in the United States of America by The Child's World®
P.O. Box 326 • Chanhassen, MN 55317-0326 • 800-599-READ • www.childsworld.com

Climbing rocks is dangerous. Even though some forms of the sport—such as bouldering—do not require ropes, no form of rock climbing should be attempted without experienced supervision.

This book is not intended as an instruction manual. Anyone interested in participating in the sport of rock climbing should begin climbing with a qualified instructor. Neither the author nor publisher of this book assumes liability for any injury or loss incurred while attempting any of the activities described in this book.

Acknowledgments

The Child's World®: Mary Berendes, Publishing Director

Editorial Directions, Inc.: E. Russell Primm, Editorial Director; Halley Gatenby, Line Editor; Susan Hindman, Copyeditor; Elizabeth K. Martin and Katie Marsico, Assistant Editors; Matthew Messbarger, Editorial Assistant; Peter Garnham, Christine Simms, and Kathy Stevenson, Fact Checkers; Tim Griffin/IndexServ, Indexer; James Buckley Jr., Photo Researcher and Photo Selector

The Design Lab: Kathleen Petelinsek, Design and Art Production

Photos

Cover: Corbis
Corbis: 5, 18, 20, 24.
Duomo/Corbis: 7, 9, 19, 28; Ken Redding/Corbis: 4, 21; Galen Rowell/Corbis: 8, 13, 15, 16; Phil Schermeister/Corbis: 12, 23; Karl Weatherly/Corbis: 27; Adam Woolfitt/Corbis: 10.

Library of Congress Cataloging-in-Publication Data

Seeberg, Tim.
  Rock climbing / by Tim Seeberg.
     p. cm. — (Kids' guides)
  Summary: An introduction to rock climbing, discussing basic techniques,
  safety measures, the necessary equipment, and popular places to climb.
  Includes bibliographical references (p.   ) and index.
   ISBN 1-59296-033-2 (lib. bdg. : alk. paper)
   1. Rock climbing—Juvenile literature. [1. Rock climbing.] I. Title. II. Series.
  GV200.2.S44 2004
  796.54—dc22   2003017802

CONTENTS

GO CLIMB A ROCK!

WHAT IS ONE OF THE FIRST THINGS

you think when you see a tree? Or a ladder? Or a wall? Even your friend's bunk bed? If you answered, "I want to climb that!" then rock climbing might be a sport for you.

In fact, hundreds of thousands of people of all ages enjoy some form of rock climbing. People scale everything from artificial climbing walls in gymnasiums to the craggy faces of steep mountains. The challenges—and rewards—of getting to the top are hard to beat.

Unlike many sports, rock climbing is without boundaries. That is, just about anyone can enjoy it. This is a sport where balance is just as important as strength.

Make sure to look up as you climb to see the way ahead.

Don't kid yourself, though. Rock climbing can be scary. It takes time and practice to move smoothly over rock. And it takes courage. If you have that courage and the determination to practice, rock climbing can be a satisfying sport. Conquering

Flexibility and patience are as important as strength in rock climbing.

a rock face can be as exciting as scoring the game-winning goal or hitting a home run. The difference is that rock climbing is as much mental as it is physical. You must think through each action before making a move. Rock climbing is also one of the few sports that lets you see right away how well you have done. There is no easy way to fake progress up a rock face, no matter how you climb it. The laws of gravity don't permit cheaters.

If you are looking for a challenge, go climb a rock!

CHAPTER ONE

SAFETY MEANS TEAMWORK

TRADITIONAL ROCK CLIMBING IS

usually done in teams. Most often, a team consists of two people, both of whom carry a few pieces of safety equipment. At any given time during a climb, one person is the leader and the other is the follower. The two teammates—or partners—sometimes trade positions throughout the climb.

The leader carries a safety rope. Safety rope is dynamic, which means it stretches to absorb the impact of a fall. One end of the rope is attached to the leader's **harness** with a strong knot. The other end is tied to the follower's harness. The leader carries various types of **protection** to place in the rock at several spots along the way. The leader clips the rope to the protection points to form an **anchor.** In order to be safe, an anchor must consist of many secure protection points.

Only one partner climbs at a time. The other—anchored to three or more pieces of protection—is **belaying.** This is done by holding the climbing rope, in case the climber slips. Belaying differs slightly, depending on which member of the team is doing it.

If the leader is climbing, the follower lets out enough rope to allow the leader to climb. As the belayer, the follower watches the leader carefully. The leader's rope is threaded through the

Ropes and a climbing harness help keep a climber safe while moving up the rock.

follower's belay device. If the leader begins to fall, the follower locks down on the rope with his or her "brake hand," which stays below the device. This stops the rope so that the leader does not fall all the way down.

When the follower is ready to climb, the leader uses the belay device. The follower then starts to climb. If the follower slips, the fall will be only as far as the slack in the rope. Often that is not more than a foot or two. This is one reason why the less-experienced climber usually goes second.

Climbers attach clips to pitons that are hammered into the rock. The clips hold supporting ropes.

On an "aid climb," climbers use ropes and protection to climb, not their hands and feet. The leader may use specialized equipment such as **holds, pitons,** or small hooks that catch on creases and bumps in the rock. The follower then gathers the protection as he or she climbs. Sport climbers use

protection that is left permanently in place on popular
rocks. Sport climbers can
also be "top-roped." In top-
roping, an anchor is placed
at the top of the wall or rock.
The rope is also belayed
from the bottom. That way, a
climber who slips should fall
no more than a few inches.
Top-roping is used at many
climbing gyms because it is
the safest and easiest way
to learn the basics of rock
climbing.

Partners communi-
cate by using certain words
as they climb. When the
leader is safely clipped to an
anchor, she will shout, "Off

Teamwork is
essential in rock
climbing. Here
the climber above
supports the
climber below.

belay!" The leader then takes the slack out of the rope between
herself and the follower. When her belay device is set, the leader
calls down, "On belay!" The follower detaches himself from his

Belaying can also be done from the ground by a partner holding a rope.

own anchor and shouts up, "Ready to climb!" The leader, now acting as the belayer, shouts back, "Climb!" Once the follower begins his first **moves,** he yells "Climbing!" to the leader, so she knows to take in rope.

Sooner or later, nearly every climber falls, but the use of ropes keeps them safe. Many of the really great climbers fall frequently because they are attempting difficult maneuvers. Climbers must learn how to fall very early in their careers. The right way to fall is with your head up and your feet under you, as if you were standing. Sometimes you have to use your arms and legs to press away from the rock or wall. This will protect your head and torso. After you stop falling, catch your breath and calm yourself. Once you feel secure, look back up at the rock, let your partner know you are ready to climb, and go for it again.

OFF TO A GOOD START

If you are new to rock climbing, you should take lessons. Beginning climbing lessons—including equipment rental—are not very expensive. Some communities even have free programs. A gym with climbing facilities and staff is the best and safest place to start climbing. Your instructor will know how to teach climbing to kids your age. Make sure to learn basic climb and belay techniques, how to tie knots, and how to communicate.

Keep these important safety tips in mind at all times:
- Never climb without protection.
- Climb within your abilities.
- Wear your helmet.
- Never climb alone.
- Always communicate clearly with your partner.
- Always double-check your and your partner's equipment before you start climbing.

CHAPTER TWO

CLIMBING STYLES

THERE ARE MANY TYPES OF ROCK

climbing. Bouldering is the most basic kind of rock climbing.

It's just the climber against the rock, with no ropes. To be done

safely, bouldering does require a **crashpad** and a trusted

spotter. It's important to remember that you should never

Low boulders can be great ways for kids to start climbing rocks. Make sure to climb with an adult.

More experienced climbers can boulder on larger rocks.

spot someone who is bigger than you. This could be dangerous for both of you.

As you might guess, bouldering involves climbing boulders. Small walls and low rock faces are also climbed, usually for practice. The heights attained while bouldering are low enough that not a lot of safety equipment is needed. Besides climbing shoes, a crashpad, and someone to spot for them, the only thing most boulderers take with them is a bag of chalk. They put the chalk on their hands to help them get a good grip on holds in the rocks. Beginning boulderers often climb while their partner positions and repositions a crashpad on the ground below them to cushion a fall. Because it takes place so close to the ground, bouldering is a good way to learn difficult moves. However, bouldering probably causes more injuries than any other type of climbing. This is because if you fall while bouldering, you hit the ground, not the end of a rope.

Free climbing is any kind of climbing where you must rely only on your hands, feet, and fingers to move up the rock. Free climbers use safety equipment, but they do not use equipment that takes away the need to use their own limbs. Sport climbers focus strictly on climbing. They do not have to worry about placing—and retrieving—protection as they go. Those pieces of equipment are permanently in place on the rock or wall so that sport climbers just have to clip their ropes into them. Sport climbing is a very popular type of competitive rock climbing.

Ice climbing is much like other forms of rock climbing. The difference is that the climber is going up ice instead of rock or plastic. Instead of using their fingers, ice climbers use special

This young climber free climbs a rock high above the ocean's roar.

tools that grab or dig into the ice. These tools include ice axes and crampons, which are metal spikes on a metal frame worn on the soles of boots.

Alpine climbers must wear more protective gear and warmer clothing while climbing at high altitudes.

Mountaineering, also known as alpine climbing, is the sport of the true mountain lover. It combines hiking and camping with ice and rock climbing. Often, mountaineers spend several nights outdoors during their trek up the mountains.

Climbing skills are a big part of mountaineering. But

there are some big differences between it and the other forms of climbing. One is the backpack mountaineers use to carry their supplies. It dramatically changes their balance. They carry both snow and ice axes and use much sturdier and heavier footwear. Mountaineers also face natural hazards, such as avalanches.

Not too long ago, a person who wanted to rock climb had to go to the mountains. Now, the mountains have come to the climbers. Well, almost. Around the world, climbing gyms have opened to make sport climbing more accessible. Climbers call it "pulling plastic" when they climb artificial courses or walls inside a gym. This type of climbing is very popular for climbers of all ages and skill levels.

YOUNG SUPERSTAR

Though she is only 21 years old, Katie Brown has been very busy. She is regarded as the world's best female sport climber. Her trophy case shows why. She has won three X Games medals for climbing (she won her first when she was 16!) and was the junior U.S. and world champion.

Katie is very small and light but enormously strong. She is known for her calm and careful approach to climbing. She seems almost lizard-like in her ability to stick to walls. Her specialty is called "difficulty climbing." In these competitions, one climber at a time attempts a wall. Whoever makes it farthest up the wall in the time allowed is the winner.

Katie has been such a success that the Women's Sports Foundation says, "She is doing for climbing what Tiger Woods is doing for golf."

CHAPTER THREE

EQUIPMENT

CLIMBING REQUIRES SPECIAL

equipment. Even though most of the basic skills used in the

different types of climbing are similar, there are important

differences in the equipment. Think of it this way: You dress

differently to walk along a beach than you would to walk across

an icy playground or a rugged trail.

At most climbing gyms, you can rent all the equipment

you need. Then, if you decide this is a sport that you'd like to get

A manmade climbing gym is a great way to practice your climbing technique.

Rock climbing gear includes special shoes, a helmet, clips and rope, and a sturdy harness.

involved in, you'll probably want to go out and buy your own gear.

A good way to get started is to buy a package that includes all the gear you'll need for rock climbing indoors, except shoes. It will consist of a harness, belay device, **carabiner,** chalk, and chalk bag.

A harness is worn for safety. It is attached to a rope to protect you from falling. You want to make sure that it fits comfortably around your waist and thighs. Go for fit, feel, and comfort—not color.

Rappeling means going down the rock face, "walking" backward as you hold a rope.

A belay device is used when **rappelling** and belaying. It is also a kind of brake. It slows and eventually stops the rope when someone falls.

Carabiners (pronounced care-uh-BEAN-ers) are handy gadgets that hook things together. You'll only need one to start out, to attach your belay device to your harness. Get a locking carabiner for safety. More advanced climbers, especially those climbing outdoors, use carabiners for hooking additional gear onto their harness.

Chalk is used on climbers' hands to give them a better grip on the rock. You can buy either raw chalk, which is a powder, or a chalk ball (less messy). A chalk bag is used to hold your chalk. It can attach to a harness or to your waist. There are various sizes.

What you wear for climbing depends on your personal preference. You can buy various types of climbing clothes—from shorts to pants to tights on the bottom, and from tank tops to T-shirts on top. Wear something comfortable that is not too **restrictive.** Light-weight material is best.

Rope is the climb-er's lifeline. Rock-climbing ropes are different from

Climbers hook extra clips to their harness. A bag at the back holds chalk that helps keep hands dry for a good grip.

those designed for caving and rescue efforts. As we said earlier, climbing rope stretches to absorb the impact of a fall. Climbing rope comes in a variety of thicknesses, lengths, and colors. Be certain the rope you use is made specifically for rock climbing. Also, carefully inspect your rope before and after each climb. Use your eyes and your fingers. If the cover, or sheath, of the rope is frayed, or if the rope feels lumpy or flat in spots, replace it. Any rope that has ever caught a climber on a severe fall should also be replaced.

Ropes are attached to the protection, which is anchored in the rock. Protection helps to keep a falling climber from falling very far. If you're the leading climber, you can expect to fall at least twice as far as your last piece of protection.

To protect your brain from falls, as well as from falling rocks, a helmet is an essential part of your safety equipment.

CLIMBING SHOES

Special climbing shoes have a sole made of a very sticky rubber material. This increases the friction between the shoe and the rock or wall, giving you much better grip while climbing. Make sure your climbing shoes fit properly and feel comfortable. The type of climbing you'll be doing will determine how stiff a shoe you'll need. Beginners should use relatively stiff shoes. Try on the shoes and make sure they are comfortably tight. You don't want the shoe to be loose or to cut off the circulation in your feet. Don't wear socks, and lace the shoes up tight.

LEARNING TO CLIMB

SOME PEOPLE HAVE SAID ROCK

climbing is like playing chess. Although many moves might

be available to you, usually only one move is the best. And

because every move you make determines the next moves that

will be available, you will be more successful if you study each

move first.

Studying the
route you will
take together up
a rock face is an
important first
step in any climb.

Three rules guide every move you will make. First, you are safest when you have the greatest amount of contact with the rock or wall. Your hands and feet are your best points of contact. At any given moment, you should be in contact with the climbing surface with at least three of these (two hands and one foot, or two feet and one hand).

This is a closeup showing an open-hand grip, one of the many ways climbers hold onto rocks during a climb.

Second, your legs are stronger than your hands and arms. Climbers always try to position themselves so their legs are supporting them and pushing them up the wall or rock.

Third, planning your climb is the only way to get to the top. Good climbers always look before they climb. They study the route, carefully planning where they want to go before they go there. They repeat this for each move, as well as for the whole climb.

In addition to following these three guiding rules, all climbers share the same basic moves. *Grips* and **jams** are two types of move. You have probably practiced two or three climbing grips without even realizing it.

The most basic grip is the *open-hand grip*. This is the same grip you might use to pick up a softball: with your hand spread, your thumb, fingers, and palm all sharing the work.

In the *cling grip*, you put your fingertips over a ledge. The cling grip can be strengthened by the downward pressure of the thumb if you place it over your index finger. This locks the index finger, and the other three fingers, into place on the hold.

In a *pinch grip*, your fingers wrap vertically around one side of a hold while your thumb presses against the opposite side. Often, your thumb has to clutch a **nub** no bigger than a pebble. Free climbers often "crack up" while they are climbing.

This does not mean they are laughing all the time (although they might do that, too). Instead, it means they use the cracks in the rock to climb. They place their fingers, hands, toes, or feet inside the openings of the rock to pull or push themselves up or hold their place. These moves are called jams.

In a *finger jam*, or finger lock, you push, then twist, your fingers into a narrow crack. The little finger is on top and your thumb is on the bottom. Sometimes this positioning is reversed, depending on the shape of the crack. The more fingers you can get into the crack, the more stable your hold will be.

A *hand jam* is used in hand-sized cracks, usually 1.5 to 3 inches (3.8 to 7.6 centimeters) wide. Some climbers who use this wear athletic tape to protect the skin on the backs of their hands.

A *fist jam* is good for larger cracks. You make a fist, but instead of punching the rock, you place your fist sideways in the crack, pinkie first. If the crack is a little wider, you can place your fist in it thumb first.

A *foot jam* is a way of using a crack in the wall or rock for a foothold. It involves putting as much of your foot into the crack as possible and then twisting your foot at the ankle to lock the jam. This is a very stable hold. *Toe jams* are for cracks where only a toe will fit.

When you climb a ladder, you usually go toe first. That

Special climbing shoes help grip rock face with the toes of your feet.

makes a lot of sense, because you can get the middle of your foot on the ladder's rung. But when you climb rocks, there may not be enough room to get even a whole toe on a hold. That is why climbers use the insides of their feet to climb. This technique is called *edging*.

Using the inside part of the foot gives a climber more control and stability. It takes advantage of the strongest part of the foot as well as the leg muscles that control it. You can test the difference yourself by holding onto a stairway banister and standing on the bottom step. Place one foot firmly in the middle

All the hard work pays off with a joyous shout and a stunning view from the top of the rock!

of the stair. Now experiment with different positions with the other foot. Is your big toe stronger than the side of your foot? Which gives you better balance? If you find edging is the best for you, rock climbing may be in your future.

The sticky soles of climbing shoes make *smearing* a very good technique when the foothold is very small or rounded. Doing a smear, the climber puts as much of the foot as possible on the hold point. The sole is smeared, or rounded, against the rock, the foot flexed upward. It is a little like pasting your foot onto the wall.

By working with an expert teacher, you can become a rock climber. You might find that it's harder to learn than some other sports. However, few sports give you both the mental and physical thrills you can get from conquering the rocks!

RESTING ON THE ROCK

Many climbers consider the rest position to be their first position. After all, resting is an important thing to learn early in your rock-climbing career. Generally, the rest position begins with finding good holds for all of your hands and feet. Next, hang off one of your hand-holds with a straight arm. Your legs should be straight and relaxed. Drop your free hand and arm down, letting them relax. Chalk up your free hand, get a good hold with that hand, then rest your other hand and arm. Everyone has a personal variation, of course, just as everyone has a favorite position for sleeping.

GLOSSARY

anchor—a place where climbers are firmly secured to the rock; many pieces of protection must be set into the rock to form an anchor

belaying—securing a climber with a rope

carabiner—a link that snaps open and shut and is used to attach rope to pieces of protection

crashpad—a large, padded mat used in bouldering

harness—nylon belts worn around a climber's waist and legs for attaching safety ropes and carrying equipment

holds—rock features that can be gripped with hands or feet; for indoor climbing, these are small grips of molded plastic bolted to the climbing wall

jams—holds made by wedging a body part into a crack in the wall

moves—the motions you make to get from one hold to another

nub—a small lump in the rock face or wall

pitons—iron spikes that climbers hammer into the rock to help them climb

protection—gear placed on the rock face or wall to help protect the climber in the event of a fall

rappelling—going down a rock or wall

restrictive—confining or limiting; wearing restrictive clothes will make you uncomfortable while climbing

spotter—someone who can help you if you fall and can protect your head and neck from injury

FIND OUT MORE

Books

Brimner, Larry Dane. *Rock Climbing.* London: Franklin Watts, 1997.

George, Jean Craighead. *Cliffhanger.* New York: HarperCollins, 2002.

Joyce, Gary. *Climbing with Children.* Birmingham, Alabama: Menasha Ridge Press, 1996.

Roberts, Jeremy. *Rock and Ice Climbing!: Top the Tower.* New York: Rosen Publishing Group, 2000.

On the Web

Visit our home page for lots of links about rock climbing:
http://www.childsworld.com/links.html

NOTE TO PARENTS, TEACHERS, AND LIBRARIANS: We routinely check our Web links to make sure they're safe, active sites—so encourage your readers to check them out!

INDEX

About the Author

Tim Seeberg is a writer based in Bend, Oregon. He has a lifelong love of the outdoors and is an avid fly fisherman. A graduate of UCLA, Tim has worked in advertising and public relations, and has also written about sports history.